Introduction
to the Introduction
to
Wang Wei

Introduction to the Introduction to Wang Wei

Pain Not Bread

Canadian Cataloguing in Publication Data

Introduction to the introduction to Wang Wei

Poems
Includes bibliographical references

ISBN 1-894078-09-8

1. Chinese poetry – T'ang dynasty, 618-907 – Adaptations. 2. Canadian poetry
(English) – 20th century. I. Pain Not Bread (Association).

PS8287.C463I57 2000   C811'.6080357   C00-930664-1

PR9195.85.C33I57 2000

We acknowledge the support of the Canada Council for the Arts for our
publishing programme. The support of the Ontario Arts Council is also
 gratefully acknowledged.

Cover art:
Pain Not Bread seal carved by Yin Guwen.
A detail from The Classic of Filial Piety, Bei Lin (The Forest of Stone Stelae), Xi'an;
photo credit: Zhao Xiangji.
Scanned images from the *Three Hundred Poems from Tang,* containing, in part, Wang
Wei's "Farewell" and a short biography.

This book is set in Mercury, Minion, Perpetua and Rotis.

Design and layout by Alan Siu.

Printed and bound by Sunville Printco Inc.

Brick Books
431 Boler Road, Box 20081
London, Ontario   N6K 4G6
brick.books@sympatico.ca

Contents

"... the state is worn away, mountains and rivers survive ..."

"... but I, though on horseback, need never return ..."

*"... hate poetry and you'll achieve high office,
love poetry and you'll vainly embrace the hills ..."*

They dress in grass, eat turnips, and despise their kings.

— written on the back of an 18th century Chinese ink
screen depicting westerners (Rijksmuseum, Amsterdam)

蒼江急夜流

Introduction to the Introduction to Wang Wei

The use and reuse of traditional Chinese poetry, with its deep-rooted doctrine of allusion. That writers created versions of classical texts, less in a process of imitation than of rewriting. Conceived as a means of honoring the masters, it was achieved through appropriation and allusion — although what appropriation and allusion there are is not necessarily, in the eyes of the critic, originality.

A paysage made new by the specific.

While the poetic project is personalized by use, the system derives
            from the forests and hills.

From willed activity: bafflement, a human voice.

Cooling Off (An Introduction to Wang Wei)

Clear waters drift through a huge mouth,
through the immensity of a tall wind.
White fish swimming in a void.
I look only in front of me.

The first line begins.
Then the moon affects the pines,
the brook moves, the bamboo crackles,
women go home,
the verbal dominance continues.
Lotuses sway, a boat meanders,
even the grass turns dry and brown.
In this poem, we should be able to read the signs.
Nature is active.
The prince, however, in those mountains,
is still. What can he do?

In some poems
Wang Wei addresses the world.

After the empty mountain
comes the evening, the full moon
is transparent. Stones burn,
bamboo trees go home
through the pines.
A prince is happy in the first line.
I know my heart is not holding me.

Uneventful Life (An Introduction to Wang Wei)

It is often written that Wang Wei had an uneventful life,
that he was a catalyst for emotions in the vein,
that he was one thing in which the world shone —
all those tempting mirrors,
erroneous, misleading, understated and serene.

In the passage of time beyond the last line,
he continues with his own exile.
Laughter and crying reflect the throat and eyes.
Twilight comes, the river races.
The undone rope gives freedom to departing friends,
paralysis to the dead city.

Now is the moment in which
the past of the future is awakening.
Knowledge leads to illumination or freedom or grief.
The sun, the stars have all gone
to their destinations.
Only time goes on,
contemplating bodies to their meaningful end.

No lover is mentioned but time —
time measured only by movement.
From one time into another condition,
from one knowledge into another uncertainty.

Autumn is far from where people live,
immersed in sand
as the cranes are immersed in ink.
I see the moon waver,
white, especially far.
The firmament ripples.
I am alone and can do everything,
yet I am not willing.
I too am immersed.

Water Chestnut Stems (An Introduction to Wang Wei)

Now that the grass is dry and brown, the written signs have been
                transposed,
so the first line begins with rain.
Afterwards comes autumn, with its evenings.
This is how we come upon the moon, that burns against the pines.
In the much-analyzed poem, we enter through a gate of dew,
and there is medicine to cool the heart.

Poems are suffering forms in which the world complains about
                the world.
Sun bakes the earth, and clouds of flame that look
like mountains rise up as the vegetation wilts.
Each line becomes the cause of some activity
that binds us to the world —
a world where, without reading, there would be no shade.

The sounds of thought are fragmentary, to be reconstructed slowly
out of the clutter of letters and symbols,
the poem's living algebra, the unidentified "you"
grown glossy with convention over time.

Out of these details — the hissing of rain, the tumult of water,
the startling of egrets, confined to the single couplet —
emerges the reader.
To meditate when a bell stirs in the mouth.
When the water chestnut stems no longer hold.
When, through the gate of the literal word-by-word rendering,
                comes the rain.

After Wandering All Day in the Old Capital, Having Reread Wang Wei's "Living in the Hills" (An Introduction to Wang Wei)

Late at night, the city walls still radiating heat,
it seems I've walked enough for the day;
I'm finally ready to leave the Old City.
The moon has risen; shadows fall across the Eastern Gate.
Far to the south the cranes are silent, having made their nests among
        the pines.
Here, too. Only the sound of branches, cooling bricks, no human
        voice.

Winter Night (An Introduction to Wang Wei)

I look in my mirror,
bright
    ashamed
        moon.
This night is endless,
the young are grass.

The shadows of plum trees, random bells,
discarded robes, a swaying pendant,
self-consciousness, the pain in which he leaves:
merely the listing of symbols, unfleshed.
We see Wang Wei through a cold winter,
a decaying tree embarrassed in elegant garments.

The full routine of his day is seen,
the lines concisely factual, records that quiver,
arched gates, high pavilions.
They never shout or despair.

But in the company of mountains
he chats and laughs, and forgets to go home —
in the constant measuring without reference.

Near death, he asked for his brush, wrote letters,
put down his brush, and died.

Night pierces the courtyards.
Shadows float officials' homes.
Sun and haze — these clerks — are gone,
yet birds sing at daybreak
and I drag my body.
I'm old. I wrote documents for heaven.

A Life of Contemplation (An Introduction to Wang Wei)

Silence is the special music. Clarified or resonant, its meaning is determined by the notes outside it — as when a bell is struck deep in the mountains, releasing the monks from contemplation, the sound dropped suddenly against the deep green of the forest, so even the adjective lengthening the duration of the moment sounds against the norm of silence. This is the silence as the mind occurs, when the mountains empty, when the mind is emptied; the phenomena have all been silenced. Then the poem escapes, and is free to move. The monks again sit rigid in the act of contemplation; Wang Wei initiates his own removal from the tangled net of his writing; the mystical translation of the terminological experience differs, is essentially the same. The metaphor of silence moves us from the world to the absence of words, to the lexical void.

Nada, ayin, wu, sunyata: when ordinary language is silenced.

To express these silences in language, use language. Let the word silence itself. Yet Wang Wei was not content: stillness signifies. We are the experience, beyond land and beyond extension. Words catch fish, the fish is caught; a secret is not compromised by analogy. The truth, if spoken, remains unsaid.

Now — decode the silent, depopulated landscape.

The Written Character (An Introduction to Du Fu)

No one knows your thoughts: the night is empty.

These translations, then, might deepen repose.

Impending violence.
And in the first line, egrets clenched like fists.
Yet "Ming" is simply "sound",
which accurately applies to the leaping fish,
the written character of relentless struggle,
an interiority impossible to reproduce,
but serene, like a flock of fists weeping on sand,
egrets sleeping in the boat's wake.

It is only in such austerity that words have weight enough to occur.

The Old Man in the Mountain (An Introduction
to Wang Wei)

The sign that unifies nature,
the absent center, the dusty world —
has led us this far.

Some readers come into the poem only twice.
A landscape is described,
and one understands in the last line
that sight has not been prepared for,
and is therefore unjustified.
A figure appears, but not with a landscape:
nature is not only what appears.

This is the failure of meaning —
no external reference or hermeneutic to unravel the world.

The bells call the fisherman and woodcutters;
the distance of the mountains
parallels the changing time of day.
The next four lines
are blown about by winds,
unable to stand, and the rice paddies
shine.

The Gown of a Dead Emperor (An Introduction to Wang Wei)

Illusory things of the phenomenal world mingle in heaven.
Egrets in sudden motion, stitched with rain.
The rain feeding the stream,
itself in sudden motion to the sea.
All causes flow seaward —
oneness, water, birds.
Poetics operating in twilight.
The single thread that leads into an open field.
A hibiscus flowering in the passing of the natural world.

The Rise and Fall of Human Breath (An Introduction to Wang Wei)

The movement and meaning of the poem
are presented through the absence of connectives;
events are simply registered, not interpreted,
the reader must do what the writer has already done:
understand the parallel movement of sound and line
that feeds the stream and startles the egrets.
The rain feeding the stream is itself created
by the evaporation of water flowing seaward.
At this point the poem seems transparent:
the water falls through the air and then passes over stones,
the waves rise and fall as do the egrets in the air.
I described a landscape, but no one understood
I was returning to my cottage through this.
It was my failure not to make unambiguous the real personal drama,
my self-immersion in a torn literary history.
And if the poem seems to be transparent,
at another level it is an artifact. Relations locked in mutability.

Grief in the last line is therefore unjustified:
the reader alone makes the poem worthy of contemplation.
I placed myself explicitly within the unravelling images,
a mountain range of symbols loosely associated with twilight:
the return to one's home, new life, the renewal of sleep.
The butterfly, the cattle, the horse, and the hawk.
All have their places, all interpretation
causes life to spin endlessly on the Great Wheel.

Now is nowhere. In my work I sought justice,
but the wise emperor disagreed —
the rise and fall of human breath becomes a long complaint;
seeing, an illusion. The transcendental is read,
the phenomena of the natural world escape,

the city carries such a cargo of pathos and longing
that daily life there vaccinates us against revelation.

Centuries later my interpreters ask,
"Can we link poem and life reasonably enough?"
Well, my son starved to death in the rebellion;
the dying sun closes my wooden door. In these lines and elsewhere,
who would not live again, if nature's order were reversed?

Variation on a Few Lines by Guan Yu (From a Painting of the Late Tang)

Surely one life should be good enough.
One life. But come autumn, the flowerheads
once more lie scattered in sleep,
like Lao Cu I bow down before clouds
and scribble nonsense in my notebooks.
I suppose salvation is always to be found elsewhere,
a blueness that's almost smoky —
I want to fill it with emotion,
the way (once) it seemed
a single word might fill the air with birds.
Seen from a distance
this desire is like a mountain range,
Guan Yu inscribing bitterly
"No thanks to the Lord of the East.
He left his name on this painting.
Though the leaves are pale,
in the end they are not falling."

Convicted of Greatness Twelve Centuries After His Death, Wang Wei is Imprisoned in a Cage of Jargon (An Introduction to Wang Wei)

Wang Wei's retreat to a pastoral landscape having become such a prime
topos (in general) that in the phrase "kong shan", the empty
mountain, we are said, at last, to have been brought into the
"presence" of a speaker.

As with the *Book of Nature* in Renaissance England, in which one comes
upon the essence of the world, although only obliquely.

The transcendental act that unifies is thus distinguished from the
incidental act in that it is an error, not an absence.

An artifact can stand as a "cartouche" for this (almost alchemical)
catalysis.

The topos of the old man, set against the empty mountain, divides the
speaker from the scene.

The distance of the mountains parallels the changing time of day.

Made lonely by the desolate landscape, he has come to his retreat.

This then is "the natural world": a rambling collage of ancient symbols,
the main system of which descends from his attachment to the
forests and the hills.

The movement of ecstasy exists, not in the passage from *enstasis* to
ekstasis, but against the figurative profusion that inhabits "silence",

the historical moment mirrored in his sudden awakening to grief and
pain.

These few lines then have become an antique mirror, in which the
right hand also becomes the left, the *anagnorissis* also a negative
epiphany.

There is some uncertainty about the next ten years of his life: at some
point he married; at some point his wife died; at some point he
acquired his estate at Wang River, perhaps after his formal return
to Chang'an.

Much of his mature poetry concerns his life here.

In the life of internal exile, beyond the pass, that which is unknown
may mean death.

Writes Du Fu:

"A breadth of hair divides wealth and utter poverty.
This strange contrast fills me with unappeasable anguish."

A Cricket's Autumn (An Introduction to Wang Wei)

The crickets recognize no human voice: no one calls.
The desolate gate and empty forest on one hand,
and white clouds on the other: dark, necessary bridge.
His whole life an appointment he has tried to keep.

But the poem ends. You and I refer to
Wang Wei and his friend Zhang Yin.
He takes Zhang's hand and
the poem has shifted into conspiracy:
we observe, vacillate once more,
looking out from our reading,
the character of his likeness.

And across the water, a cricket's autumn
falls on a thatched hall. White clouds call no one.
I dare not inflict myself on this,
seeing all the peopled world at the end of your hand.

Another Universe (An Introduction to Wang Wei)

More real than the real, more false
than the false, the secret of appearances.
No fables, no narratives, no compositions.
No scenes, no theater, no action. Forget all this.

The detritus of social life, the slight figuration of objects
scattered in the randomness of appearance.

The void, then absence, of the political realm,
reappearances that haunt its emptiness.
An acute, almost metaphysical seduction
deriving from the nullification of the real,
from the unreal inversion of these haunted objects.

Only objects without referents, out of context:
these old newspapers, these old books, these old nails.
These old boards. These scraps of food ghostly in their deinscription —
A lost reality like the aroma of a previous life
that still haunts our consciousness.

No landscapes, no skies, no natural light;
no faces, no psychology or history. Everything is a backdrop,
everything an artifact. Even suspense, fragility, obsolescence.
Even the insistence on the letter and the mirror —
those lost, distant signs of a transcendence vanished into the quotidian,
a worn plank whose knots and rings, without hands, tell time.

These are things which have already transpired,
in a time which has already occurred.

There are no fruits here, no meats or flowers,
nature is carnal, a casual arrangement on a horizontal plane
like the ground or a table. Everything is in suspense:
even light and perspective
are signs of a slight vertigo,
of an appearance previous to reality.

This mysterious light without origin,
whose rays are no longer real,
this shallow pool of water floating in the distance.
Perhaps death illuminates all things directly.
A shadow that doesn't elongate at sunset, or with time.

And if there is a miracle, it is never achieved —
like painted grapes so real birds peck at them.

Another universe whirls forward, with nothing behind it.

Every Shade of Friendship (An Introduction to Wang Wei)

Another universe whirls forward, with nothing behind it.
One sets out to go beyond life,
then goes not "beyond life" but without it.
We are alive, but I was shaken by death.
My wife, my mother. No formula for affection,
no lilacs. But I loved you in disgrace and rain,
in the palace warfares, in the countryside.
Every shade of friendship persists,
in the mountains, in the grass,
in the vast Gobi desert
where yellow sands blot out the frontier
of particular feelings and attachments.

Credo: Deep South Mountain   (An Introduction to Wang Wei)

No sutras, no hymns, no doctrine,
but nature with its personal implications.
A landscape is described, and one understands
in his returning to his cottage the invisible presence
of rapids, the hissing, the tumult,

are not to be interpreted.
Ambiguity is the necessary language of nature.
Twin streams falling from a great height,
virtually inarticulate, alive in the forest.

And Wang Wei? We see him
bowed down by duty and mountains,
the resignation to new systems of uncertainty.

As Buddha sat silent in a famous instant,
or a clock exists in deep unmeasured space,

he has become a convention. Nonetheless, he persists.

Continuous Elegy (An Introduction to Wang Wei)

Time's diction is a wave of self-immersion,
a declaration of the present in the hissing of the rain.
This statement, in a purely honorary time,
is neither meaningful, nor wholly meaningless,
and baffles my commentators,
so the point of that allusion, after all, is lost.
是 甚 麼 的 意 思 ﹕"is-what's-meaning?",
as opposed to "meaning what?".
I envy that apparent clarity,
the brief transparent whiteness of a world
made visible by rain.
Now I see blossoms speeding in the woods,
the present as a sword. Too late,
I see I've gestured only at the moment's tomb.

As Buddha Did (An Introduction to Wang Wei)

Words fail as Buddha did,
as John of the Cross in his allegories,
Jesus in the parables,
Kafka in the nightmares.

By now we can decode the familiar,
and separate from the human world.
I sprawl on a big rock,
I gargle with water and wash my food.
Who could know there are human affairs in the valley?
The ultimate goals are the common goals.
When we hear a bell in a deep ravine,
the ravine is audible.

There is a last aspect of Wang's life.
A farewell letter, a further interpretation, an essay in praise.
History has been generous in the preservation of silence.
Among the silences, the one he chose himself is the one most often
         heard.
It is, obliquely, experience:

On straw mats we eat pine nuts,
as day leaves I light the lamp.

Time passes.
There is one last remembrance of that other life.

Han River (An Introduction to Wang Wei)

An old catalogue, a portrait,
an island in the Han River.
With these he appears to console himself.
The river flows,
time flows daily into the east.
Embarrassed, in elegant robes,
he asks for little — or nothing.
The life of the unwilling bureaucrat,
his real life on the Wang River.
Once more in the fierce ambiguity
he vacillates.
But legend is closing his wooden door.
Will he ever live again in our presence?
We are uncertain how to witness the darkness and promise.

Silk Route (An Introduction to Wang Wei)

History, like any musical notation, has been generous in the preservation
          of silence.
The ecstatic journey out of Turkestan, a saurian landscape inhabited by
          winds —
first two steps and then another, by way of the Silk Route into China,
late in the Tang Dynasty, An Lushan. The court musicians forced to play
at Frozen Emerald Pond. From a faltering mind we see
a paradise, the lost transcendental, the leaves of the scholar tree
falling on the empty palace, disaster and death.
The musicians play with tears in their eyes.
What is the meaning of the song?

Wang River (An Introduction to Wang Wei)

Twilight, the river, a late mirror.
A historical future mirrored in the moment
the river races away.

The river races away.
The movement of bodies to their meaningful end.
No lover is mentioned.

Friendship (An Introduction to Wang Wei)

What if the words Wang Wei now are only a temple?
Or a lodge where one spends the night,
drinking and talking, limited, as always,
to the limited events of one's life.
A little asocial joy,
the impish hyperbole of friendship —

that one sets out expectant, lucky to be here —
yet all experience is essentially the same,
a sad whistling among the intellectuals. So,
if Wang Wei is an inn then, the inn a resting place,
the moon an ornament, the forest rain —
perhaps our talents blind us after all.

To find it is the old man, elegantly dressed,
and usually so proper in demeanor,
who has made his way between the tables, slightly tipsy,
upsetting the winecups of those engaged in
otherwise quite serious debate.

One More Bowl of Wine (An Introduction to Wang Wei)

You and I — we are the only ones left alive.
The mountains are remote,
beyond them only strangers.
Why not drink another bowl of wine?

Outside — only past and future:
mountains and rivers, drums and horns.
Unknown dangers spring up wildly and crowd the roadway.
Why not drink another bowl of wine?

The consolations of life are in the drinking bowl.
In friendship's tangle of rising factions.
Why not leave your coat and stay awhile. See?
Already another conflict is brewing.
Why not drink another bowl of wine?

Worldly Noise (An Introduction to Wang Wei)

Full of movement, season, aroma,
the meadow is alive.
In the green life of companionship,
invisible harmonies decorate
the everyday clamor.
The finality of dying closes the wooden door.

That green life — and now it passes —
whose vacillation carried
such pathos and longing.
Order is paralyzed.
The river flows.

But in the hills I walk and, for a time it seems, am happy.
The moral shadows
set out from the empty island.
Caught on the shoals of language
they become another form of memory.

Worldly noise! You lead us to the precipice,
although we say we are beyond language.
Words are like fishtraps. Or twilight,
when sensation, like the river,
is flooded with night's ink.

國破山河在

Storm Lanterns (A Variation on Some First Lines by Du Fu)

Half my hundred-year life gone —
yet borderlands return to no one. Autumn comes.
Above the tower: a lone, twice-sized moon,
a cloud-formed village.
In a town to the north, a watchman's
final light on the water.
Storm lanterns.
A river moon cast only feet away.
A bamboo chill drifts through the bedroom.

I row upstream past the tower,
a slight rain comes.
A thousand feet up, along sheer silk,
a traveller from southern darkness,
at the edge of heaven, descends.

In the city, night's five brief watches begin.
I step out for a moment, then back.
I remember long ago slipping away.
It is bitter cold, and late, and falling.
Looming rain and restless wind.

Our thatch house perched where land ends.
Roads not yet glistening, rain slight.
War carts have ended all travel,
the lamp gutters and flares.
Rivers and mountains survive broken countries.
The Dual Principles have ended in wind and rain.

The last watch sounds, then, in Guizhou.
Standing alone, austere, among the willows,
beyond the smoke and dust,
travelling again in some distant place,
my sad eyes find frost and wild blooming.

Sky (From the Late Tang)

All words contain the radical for sky.
The stations of perspective fading into incandescence,
all the civil ordering of night,
the stately presence of the cities of the plains appearing,
like the Milky Way, obscured by dust,
from all the years of loathing and of empire.

The slow, inevitable decline begins, ill-omened,
but with a delicate 9th century manner.
The difficult critiques of policy, the rigors of dissent,
discarded like a fan, without shame,
flattery being the element which travels best,
stricter of form, with more fidelity to human diffidence.

The shadow of the coming decade rises with a clash of sound,
uncertain as the first patterns of song emerging out of water, without
                    definition.
Barbarians, in phalanx, touring the Great Wall
which is, therefore, neither past nor present.
Twice opened, the chrysanthemums, resembling
older, wiser heads that have refrained from making choices
that are meaningless. They see the lone boats set out,
though my own version eludes me.

No future exists (i.e. in the collective sense) for a nation
whose idiom has grown entangled with its own mythology.
The general, day-to-day currents may perhaps continue,
dense patterns of abundance and counterpoint,
concrete as water, flowing,
milky, after rain,

or hissing like white silk — all that is purely transitive —
but no pure recollection,
only the uneasy conscience of syntax, pointing north.

Disintegration, finally, fuses past and present.
The sudden scales of history and dissidence.
Sky on sky.
But real time exists elsewhere, folding
and looping backwards on itself,
the rare free variations,
all the obscure years of bitterness and exile —
of that other, civil, scale — like a window
where exorcised demons stand
weeping blood into the red of the chrysanthemums
and, seeing this, Li He takes up his brush.
A Tatar horn, he begins, *tugs at the north wind.*
North of their tents surely is the sky's end.

Introduction to Du Fu

Ambiguity, calculated or generative, as a means of discontinuous
  organization, at first seemingly familiar to us,
comes in time to exceed the bounds of traditional decorum.
The claim of engagement as a form of praise for existence.
But the restrictive density of certain stereotyped hardships comes to
  preclude radical innovation.
The "poetry of things", with its composed simplicity;
and, of course, the monumental corporeal distortions of social
  realism and quasi-surreal introspection.
A class whose very *raison d'etre* is to administer government,
  therefore, suffers grief by implication,
the metaphysical displacement of ceaseless worry over political
  affairs in which barbarian armies come to embody the
  metaphysical abyss.
When empathy surpasses decorum, the shape of the spirit becomes
  decimated, increasingly foreign in repose.
Pared to an absolute minimum, stripped of grammar,
a caesura, surely, divides a disposition toward action from that of a
  faith in ultimate order.
The resulting contrasts follow certain moral geodesics, the
  threatening tension between predator and prey in which an
  egret, for example, may be seen as rising from the river
  like a clenched fist.
In Chinese, the ideogram "ming" contains both "bird" and "mouth",
  but means "sound".

"Ming". The fish jumping. The egret startled out of sleep.
Language is defined by usage; every word is allusive, to some
  extent.
Buried, finally, 43 years after his death, returned to the family
  graveyard near Luoyang,
Du Fu's wanderings did not end with death.
If my words are not startling, he wrote, *then death itself is
  without rest.*
*By November, the rivers will be steady and smooth again
and a light boat will come to carry me anywhere.*

A Little Primer of Du Fu (An Introduction to Du Fu)

Anything on wheels will serve
to take the temper of the times,
the quotas marched back from the provinces
who sit and smoke beside the road
to let the guns, on heavy cradles, lumber past,
and in the capital, the
fashionable ladies picnic in the park,
historians acquire their accents,
not without a tone of gentle mockery.
Everything exists beyond the limits of its stated reasons,
though perhaps in a corrupt and fragmentary state.
Newly despondent over having had to give up wine,
I feel compassion shrinking
to a landscape of my own dimension.
I wish this to be recorded with its irony intact,
Du Fu's account of his encounter with the
hunted prince being
difficult to read for nuance,
royal fiascos, like other royal architecture,
facing south, toward their antecedents.
These are the branches which once symbolized a brilliant past,
the heights of luxury that leave a man
unable to undress himself —
he stands before the huge pavilions,
casting shadows on the vaults and thinks
them like the sky, until the river trembles
and the sacraments are given:
safety, order, measurement,
the path held up before him like a painted mirror,
but the image is inverted,
played out on some unknown surface
where a servant smooths
the freshly folded linen, artisans with
calloused hands continually lift and plane,
until the beams and rafters come to an end,

then hang there,
leafless, stricken,
in the dusty shafts of light that
filter through the half-completed anteroom,
the body of an ant that crosses filled with agate,
hope is buried amid fierce rivers,
An Lushan. The polis crumbles into chaos.

Now — late spring again, becoming evening.
When I name that era,
everything departs, or heads toward disorder,
grass is growing on the steps,
and utter stillness reigns.
Such separation startles the heart.
Dusk no longer brings the clouds of dust
raised by barbarian horsemen.
Overhead, uncertain what may yet be in debate,
the floating clouds, oblivious, drift by all day.

Mountains and Rivers (An Introduction to Du Fu)

I hear the country swallowing its sounds.
In the riverside palaces, a thousand doors
lock up the greenness of the new spring's rushes.
Mountains and rivers ruined by the state
survive, though barely. Why should spring
still bother turning green?
I remember the rainbow banner
that used to end south of here,
and the park within all things
that put forth color.
There was a palace in each person.
Maids of honor carried bows and arrows,
white horses chomped on yellow metal.
If you bent back to face the sky
you could bring down clouds
Laughter brought down rain.
Now the toll of industry keeps wandering souls
from returning. Clear water flows only
in remote places, though neither the one
who stayed nor the one who went
have any news of it at all. It's human enough
to cry over this. How can rivers,
water, and flowers end? The city's covered
with the dust of an artificial twilight.
I can only look north, and pin my hopes
on the loyal grasses,
that once went on forever.

The Language of War (An Introduction to Du Fu)

Endless facets in the fields of meaning glitter but ruin the eyesight:
mountains small enough to fit into a single glance,
days drunk and singing.
Rarely a distinction between the public and private graces.

Outside the implements of war clatter and creak.
Always some clerk to scare up men and send them out,
virtually inarticulate in the fervor of the day's
acute distillation.

What is "appropriate", as always, is defined by circumstance.
The density of composed simplicity.
The spectre of detachment from impending violence,
whose political entropy is in a

suddenly restricted realm of utterance — apparent empathies, in form,
that are abuses of "the personal",
whose very *raison d'etre* is the
re-creation of a mindless, public,

(if traditional)
decorum behind which
the functionings of
government continue.

Nothing remains in that sense of meaning but "civilization", the illusion of
            civilization
whose absolute order is an article of despair in faith,
the *a posteriori* resignation to consensus whose manner of speaking
offers freedom from the unseen, threatening, outer world.

Against this, only individual words have weight enough to occur:
river, war — the endless fields of meaning.
All language is defined by usage.
"The killing must be kept within limits."
A country is nothing without its borders.

The Constellations (An Introduction to Du Fu)

A man's life is not-seeing another's life —
like two constellations,
one always rising while the other is setting,
Rigel, Betelgeuse, and Bellatrix in Orion;
and the two unnamed stars, one perhaps Antares
and the other Wei, in Scorpio. This evening then,
what is evening but the sharing of lamp light?
Youth's vigor doesn't last.
Temples turn grey,
and half my friends are ghosts.
Those twenty years walk the halls.
Sons and daughters form sudden rows
tapering away in every direction,
every one a question-and-answer being.

Night rain cuts the spring chives;
rice, cooking, mixes with yellow millet.
But friendship never empties.
We are always separated from tomorrow
by mountain peaks; and the world's affairs,
on both sides, are lost to sight.

Sixty Days of Rain (From the Late Tang)

Sixty days of rain pour down onto the ruined crops,
then brilliant sunshine, autumn,
and the sound of clothes for cold weather
being pounded on washing blocks.

The papers bring old news:
the Yangtze Gorges will be flooded,
the willows of the Han capital
pounded to dust by a thousand years.

Nothing is sacrosanct, nothing, anymore,
purely intransitive. The weight of syntax,
as meticulous as silk — but nothing we can learn from,
nothing we depend on any longer.

Everywhere the constructions of daily life, of daily history,
are taken to be obvious —
the characters for woman, surname, heart, entering the commentary,
carry residues of pattern, structure —

but the ideas themselves
pass without shadow,
without form, aspect, weight —
except the present,

the terracotta horsemen suddenly compressing time
into a single word.
A line beginning
"Dog. Bark. Water."

And on the water
Li Bai once more steps toward the moon,
the story in the reconstruction
rigid and elaborate as a sonnet,

an object of veneration
hung out in the weather
of a culture constellated around the great names
because there is no other axis.

Then the page begins and sixty days of rain
pour down onto the ruined crops again.
After, brilliant sunshine,
autumn,

and the sound of clothes for cold weather
being pounded on washing blocks
amidst a green so terrible
it hurts the eye.

A world like this is sometimes possible — undisfigured by sentiment.
That puts one foot after the other, and despairs without repetition.
My home, begins Li Bai, is at dusk. When the sound of wind is in the
               leaves,
and one may soften, but not abolish, its indifference.

A Dream (An Introduction to Du Fu)

Death eventually means an end to tyrants,
life means anguish without end in the pestilential country.
No news. But an old friend entered my dream,
meaning that now the net's been tossed over you
and even your wings won't do you any good.
I'm afraid that my dream is of a not-living soul
and a not-to-be-measured road. You can't journey
back and forth in your sleep over that kind of distance,
a soul permanently detached from its body,
or a body permanently detached from its soul.

It was in the light, and so the maple woods were green.
Then a shadow darkened them.
Before it sank the moon filled my roof,
and with it, the still doubtful shine of your face.

Spring (An Introduction to Wang Wei)

Now it is spring, and

a boat will come from the south, plowing upstream.
Birds will float behind the mast,
and misty reeds make clouds in water.
I'll ask you where you're going,
and you'll say you are a failure going off to hibernate
among the mountains. The cities will become
invisible. Fields will darken.
Herds will graze in drizzle.
I'll see your bright coat vanishing,
and among seasonal plants,
insects will clamor and spiders sing from beams.
Feelings are eternally sprouting from the world.
I'll lie in this corner of heaven and watch
the mountains hiding remotely in that endless blur.

Good Daughter (An Introduction to Du Fu)

Our generation is like a fine lady living in obscurity
in some now-emptied valley. We say to ourselves
that we were good daughters of good families,
but the truth is that for us fortune hides in the grass,
and that year after year has fallen to some advancing rebel army
no high office could have protected us from.
I can't find either the bones or the flesh
of the period we were born into. I don't know
whether to say that the world's feelings are decayed,
or that it feels a kind of hatred for everything that's finished.
But that kind of hatred flickers like an oil lamp
with each passing breeze. Every husband's fickle,
and thinks a new woman is as beautiful as jade.
Well, there are trees here whose leaves fold up at night,
as if they know it's time. I see new women's smiles
in old women's weeping. I suppose you'll say
that intellectuals are always patching holes in the roof
with some still-living vine, that this
is the sort of amateurish and ineffectual thing
one can always imagine them doing once it's too late,
in their thin blue sleeves,
when the weather is already turning cold,
and the evening is searching for someplace
to lean its long bamboos.

Dreaming of Li Bai (An Introduction to Du Fu)

All day the floating clouds move overhead;
all day, but they never arrive. For three nights I've dreamed of you.
I see your mind — kindly, but with a leave-taking
that's always hurried, and sometimes you'll say

it's not easy to come to you this way.
The rivers and lakes are always stirred up by wind,
the little boat's oars by which I pull myself towards you each night
grow as long in the water as my fears.
They sink into blackness, and I can't move anymore.

I wake up then, and go outside to scratch my white head.
I'm left feeling as though I've been disappointed
in something terribly important, as though my life
had just been poured away down some well.
Heaven's mesh is supposed to be wide,
but my growing old still got caught in it.
I couldn't slip through. Did you?
This year has seen a thousand autumns already
but still it won't die — or go see
the Medical Examiner for its own post-mortem.
And you — I thought you were the biggest fish of all.
Now I dream of you afraid to tumble from your own boat.

Sleep (From the Late Tang)

The blossoming of shadows on the inner walls
slowly turns into evening. The stars look down
on a myriad of unmoving doors. Unable to sleep,
you hear the wind, and imagine jade bells
that announce the arrival of minor officials, dismounting hurriedly
on their way to morning audiences with the emperor.
But tomorrow morning is still sealed business.
Between now and then you'll frequently ask yourself
what night is truly like,
how it ever came to be this long, or this dark,
and for just one moment you'll see that blackened sky,
so much bigger than you ever imagined:
a piece of paper unfolding nine times
until it blocks out everything.
No wonder the stars look down on us,
and run so quietly on their rails.
Don't sleep then. Listen to what you only imagine:
metal on metal, jade bells,
papers being opened —
and then sleep.

A History of the Late Tang

Technology, government, art, thought —
the century deepens.

Year after year the new leaves grow,
yet I have grown old. I wake early,

more each day. Life is remarkably literal.
Once I would have wanted

to be wrapped up and carried in her sleeve.
That place where we loved —

how the night grass hid its symmetry.
That our clothes might be laundered by dew and snow ...

Unlovely objects, tell me.
You cannot turn away.

The doctors say that too much passive
sadness is bad for the heart,

but I haven't the skill to
read these thoughts anymore.

Perhaps I should get up and go then.
Not wait for the berries to ripen, and you to leave me.

Old Prose (From the Late Tang)

Consensus is reluctance. The day is over,
at least for this troubled age. On the news
old men are glimpsed by old men;
frost and snow are sent in taxes to the capital.
Illusory, the past — in fact, cliché.
Nothing was what it is.
In the boardrooms and ministries
where poise is invented,
in the meticulous pidgin of the ruling elite,
in the rank-and-file sent journeying
to the end of language,
the day is over.
Consensus is reluctance.
At least for this troubled age.

Who are you, ghost?

Whichever road you choose
you lose your way.

Burning Murals (From the Late Tang)

Among maids burning murals of ancient heroes,
a hundred years of the saddest news,

the swift allegiances of time
are smoke, then gone.

The games — of sport and war —
both lost and won in turn.

In the autumn evening
there are no great men.

Seeing that pleasure costs more than regret,
I content myself with watching the fine rain, alone.

Peace Road Mountain (An Introduction to Du Fu)

Autumn is the home of departure, a joyous banishment,
the formidable road with its unknown duties

that rises vertical a hundred miles south of here,
where summer is warmth still to the ripening plums.

The instant before sleep the soul drifts off, as Du Fu says,
into the blue empyrean, with letters for the dead —

those breaths of form whose lives burn on
in their resemblance to our lives.

But autumn is returning to Youzhou again,
sailing south along Dongting Lake,

and Du Fu once more begins the journey
north, toward Chang'an.

Heroes! Peach trees! Six days of rain
in that winter of the quiet grave.

Du Fu
is dead.

And already the ancestors of the *koto*
are burning paper on the first day of spring.

Bitter Heart (An Introduction to Du Fu)

Bitter heart, you that dwell unseen
as those horses long ago,
whose likeness is presumed
in literature and silks, know this:
how like lightning, up and down, flashing over the bridge —
or vain and lovely as the sound
of sunwhite swans, this life of ours.
To go now, with spring for a companion.
Each of us greying at the temples.
Fame too: such a little man, with a balding head!

Cloud Music (An Introduction to Du Fu)

At the age of forty-one:
sets out on the dark bridge
from one personality to another —
in this very body to wake and live.

A rose has no counterpart;
good deeds, changelessness ...
somehow these poems, copied on the back of the head
(meaning death) survive.

By now the moral shadows are gone.
The open secret is friendship.
Now I hear cloud music,
stirring even the beautiful clouds.

我雖跨馬不得還

The Transmission of Salt (An Introduction to
Li Bai and Du Fu)

The original plums were
green rather than blue —
an older narration,
a longer separation —
but it is no longer possible to return to that Chang'an,
the long marches and years of toil,
three armies brought to their knees,
for what?

An Lushan   the great rebellion —
fifty million in the census previous,
and after, seventeen. Chaos and hunger on the roads.
The Yellow River flowing to the sea.

I read again and late spring
floods the characters.
Domestic insights, patriotic sentiments,
narratives of separation, war,
departure, loss. Exposed to these
the poem resembles salt,
the product of negotiation, arbitration, compromise.

From so great a distance,
centuries and cultures drift apart.
Small protests that occasioned famous visits,
a passing commentary on the tax on salt,
the bitterness of exile, from an outpost
of the fading empire, in the letters of a minor bureaucrat
that catch us by the sleeve —

I write these words at random
on a torn silk shirt:

> *Along the road that leads toward Luoyang*
> *the willow pollen, blown like snow,*

has filled the air again.

Witty and elegant, the floating clouds
obscure the sun.

All day I see my friends set out across that bridge
and know I will not see them safe again.

Translation (An Introduction to Du Fu)

Hope is not tied to the heart
but travels alone homeward,

dwarfed by repetition.
I am tempted to write "The willows of the Han

capital ..." but that mood of despair
belongs to a later period,

and would be ambiguous in the wrong way,
suggesting either a past day, or today,

and the day should be either past or future,
or both, blurred by water,

by rain tapping idly on a skin drum.
The danger, as always, is in taking

this to be a kind of knowing,
the reed blossoms to be blue, rather than white.

And what of the faulty
English by which

Li Bai sets off in his boat
at sunset? A few strokes as the water makes

the radical for heart, and then
the voice beginning

*For more than a year now, for one reason or another,
I have written nothing which deserves printing.*

The Shadows of Plum Trees (An Introduction to Du Fu)

Faith is nothing but the abyss come to life,
the sound of marching armies

and despair's creation of
pathetic forms of reason.

Only mountains should judge the dead,
but what if their greenness never ends?

The language of the present
is the present.

Age, influence, gender, class —
all are altered beyond recognition.

Yet the river of allusions flows,
and meaning flows daily to the east.

An empty island will always be associated
with those who lived here.

My friend is gone,
who now, I see, is only grass, and lilacs.

The News (An Introduction to Du Fu)

All the news today is wet. Wet soil, wet earth.
A decade's turmoil simply ended.
Someone turning on their heel on the sodden turf.

Like little black and white counters on a board
surrounding one's opponent's men,
flowers hurt the visitor's heart,

and all night long a bugle sounds.
One mood succeeds another swiftly then —
elation followed by awe,

awe by a sense of isolation,
isolation, loneliness,
then loneliness by patriotic worry, fear

I'd like to go for a walk,
but everywhere I go the news is with me,
blowing hard against my forehead,

making me shiver, soaking me to the skin.
Everything, I know, is in this predicament.
The way the lights come on,

or cars hiss past, weeping in the rain.
Heaven and earth, day and night
are split.

The Clouds (An Introduction to Du Fu)

This way, barbarians, if you want to return to obedience!

Broken courage has been not-yet-summoned-up
into the souls it could inhabit —

the not-yet-supremely-honored-ones, without talent,
the daily more old and decrepit. Reality that, smaller than an ant,

each day must surmount the most extreme summits,
climbing up toward the layered clouds,

the end of beauty, with its terrifying concentration.
But all appearances are gorgeous thoughts:

late spring shines like embroidered silk cloth,
and the sky hangs down past your hairline like a blue band.

Turning, what is it that, all along,
has been concealed behind your own back?

Only firmly fitting clouds pressing pearls against aprons,
the purple camel-hump emerging from the green cauldron,

rhinoceros-horn chopsticks,
and a belled knife vainly cutting threads,

the flying steed that passes overhead but never stirs the dust,
while the imperial kitchen sends out in succession

the eight precious foods, meant to honor the
barbarian generals, but they recoil in horror.

Meanwhile, the sound of flutes and drums accompanies
the moving of the gods;

great countries granted as titles
are passed from hand to hand, like pepper pots across a tabletop.

To have followers thronging truly is the path to power.
But after arriving by horse, doesn't everything seem to dawdle

even as it advances? The rider dismounts in front of the balustrade
and enters the patterned carpet. The willow down

buries everything: it's snow, and water-weeds,
and the bluebird flies off bearing a red handkerchief.

This way indeed, barbarians, if you want to return to obedience:
so many cold hands that will never be warmed by having power,

whole armies marching into death
without moving a muscle,

clouds that, in the end,
must bow to the inevitable,

and the mind that approaches suddenly is without anger.

Fragmentary Impromptu (From the Late Tang)

Wood. Dark. General. Grass.
Bow, drawn. White, wind.
The Wall is understandable only as water.
The sky swallows the road to Kokonor.
Various lucky accidents make it possible to render a thousand miles
of moonlight with perfect literalness.
The sacrifice of reticence,
the gradual precession of the intellect.
Transparent waters in the autumn season,
smoke and yellow grasses.

Snow-Viewing Room (An Introduction to Wang Wei)

Polished and brown, the leaves of early autumn fall.
Reedy and grey, the waters of the icy lake abrade.
Rules may be written as I sit obediently
and receive instruction at the feet of time,
but I am not despairing over this life alone.

Friends look back and mourn the passing
of another world, imagining it reached a greater,
or, compared to ours perhaps, less troubled height —
an awe before the moon and stars,
a splendor reflected by birds.

But such beauty is always virtual.
The coarse laughter of peasants
on their way to the threshing ground
offends the sensibility of
ladies in their hand-embroidered silks,

and vice versa.
All feeling must carry this cargo.
Cut loose from the moorings, adrift,
I see the night begin to fall — a moving brush —
and then the firmament is ink.

Crows (An Introduction to Du Fu)

White-headed crows have welcomed autumn to Chang'an.
They strut and caw and peck at people's rooves:
you'd think they were barbarians, advancing on the city's heights
to prise loose everything and carry off their plunder.

This world is too beautiful to be true
and too beautiful not to be true:
tonight the year's evening's short light
frosts the edge of heaven.

Sons and daughters spring up, and the endless line of
sons and daughters, growing and departing, brings a sense
of joy and quiet desperation. The raucous crows,
the jaundiced mirror that reflects all the world —

Just standing straight, just feeling, for a moment,
all the weight of that indifference,
can be hard labor.
But maintenance is the spirit's job:

to make the beams and rafters turn their heads
and see what a great weight it is that they must
carry for another year — though nothing is preserved,
in truth, beyond the likeness of divided empires,

the sight of ministers, their diligence forever pointed upward,
scurrying like clouds before the cool, northwest wind
that heralds autumn and the stations of an
endless chain of well-appointed meeting rooms.

The moon emerges like a momentary glimpse
of something white and snowy as the distant Snowy Mountains,
the previous, declining year still winding its brocade
around the always-newly-out-of-style pavilions,

the gloomy secluded paintwork where the young are gathering,
though amiably enough,
to prise loose what has taken maybe
half a lifetime in the making. I, myself, remember this,

though supposedly it is forgetting that is universal.
But I have forgotten humanity and justice,
and that was not enough. I have forgotten the rites and their music,
and even that is not enough.

The world already marvels at so many
with so many designs on it, so many plans
to embellish it against its will.
But life does not depend on truth (as we are often told).

Actually, it doesn't take a carpenter to make a thing of wonder.

Drunken Battles (An Introduction to Du Fu)

No painting can tell you what age is going to arrive —
not even if riches are already drifting in around your ears
like geese returning noisily each spring.
The present is like petty cash for those perpetually honored by time,
but for the stableboys, it's always melancholy.
So what if we're "summoned to presence"?
Each day the posters and manifestos were plastered up across the city —
and look what happened to them.
The various generals went to work with their brushes
opening up new appearances like hucksters promoting worthy hats.
How fierce their waists grew! I wouldn't change a whisker
of those drunken battles. Everyone looked grim and bold,
and brandished Jade-flower manes in place of real opinions.
I guess the truth is painters, like mountains, never stay the same.
Remember that room in the palace we entered once?
The painted horses quickly exhausted every shape,
until eventually we had to fall back on stock images
just to be able to see them again — pathetic really,
like those people out walking the roads
who'll never be the subject of a portrait,
never so much as "lift the door-knocker of greatness".

Even in its desperate straits, though,
the world is never totally impoverished.
The day leads up red steps to where
a small wind issues from the palace gate,
like generals spreading white silk on command,
wasting their craftsmanship painfully planning more mist.
But sometimes it does actually happen,
to everyone's amazement, the dragon actually emerges
and, in one wash of ink, blanks out a myriad of ages.
Only no painting can tell you when that day is going to arrive.
Until then, everyone goes on looking grim and bold,
and summoned to presence.
But, as I've just said, they're all stableboys,
and so to them, it's always melancholy.

Breath (An Introduction to Du Fu)

Books should begin and end in pleasure.
The breath that was referred to as
war or loneliness, or poverty or loss,
could equally well be spoken of as friendship,
love, or wine. The range of meanings
is not important, so long as we can get together
every week or so,
make these small protests against our own characters
and, like teasing feathers from an ancient pillow,
find out what it is that might be in our minds. That way,
whatever is found is valuable.
Perhaps the centuries part, and feelings are transmitted —
even if, in the final analysis,
each poem is the product of endless
negotiations and compromise.
The syntax then takes on a formal quality,
though moderated, one hopes,
by a colloquial diction, an openness
to irony and humor, all of which
might break up the self-imposed
isolation of the poem.
That way, when the visitor comes to the small cottage
on the border of misanthropy and hyperbole,
we can open the door and say "C'mon in.
Let's have a few drinks together
and get quietly hammered."

Lazy Afternoon, Thinking About Certain Famous Lines From the Late Tang

Every spring I've become more and more allergic to the world,
hacking and sniffing, unable even to complain decently,
like some minor artist, unknown even in his own day.
Now, it seems, reprieved at last by laziness,
I'm no more to be found among the many chasing fame —

the afternoon lies absolutely open,
like those gardens of the Old Japan
whose aim was said to be
"to capture with the sky..." —

and I would sometimes, too, I think,
like to capture something of that scale — something
large and unimaginably diffident — the sky for instance.
But to capture with what? The net, the rod, the octopus trap,
or some similar device in words?

From my little patch of hillside
I can watch the huge blue sky revolving over what was once Chang'an,
and see the past is endlessly divided.
Wang Wei, Du Fu, Meng Jiao.
Li Bai, Du Mu, Li He.
Idlers and whiners —
with the odd bureaucrat thrown in for good measure.
Full of ambition, though I know that
no one knows their accents anymore —

Still, seeing the pines planted here may be those they sat under,
those they spoke to, I let myself imagine it so, and feel, guiltily,
there may yet be some pleasure to be gained
sitting here listening to the murmur of their boughs on a windy day.

Still Evening (An Introduction to Du Fu)

In front of this world, another world should be placed,
so that an occasional breeze might tinkle the bells
that hang from the four-cornered eaves of the cosmos ——

"In front of this world", I think ——

and idly turning the page
I realize, without haste,
I've wasted my day.
Between my gateposts
the city's lights have come on,

and temple bells, like sad belled cats,
forever chasing mice.

A peaceful night: the scent of tamarisk orders the world,
half-deserted office towers, their vastness
honeycombed with cubes of light.

Toward the distant hills, the taillights of a
single car ascend.

Moon emerges cold, as Du Fu says,
above the naked suburban plain.

What is this great weight?

Forbidden City (After the Late Tang)

Green grass swallows the greener air
and, seeing this, the scholar lays down her brush.

Drifting on thought all day — the old cloud pattern's
convolutions, wrought in marble,

that recall a fabled emperor,
while the imperial craftsmen remain unknown.

In less than two years, how much I've changed:
less hurried, more tired.

The world of opinion passes, leaving what? —
the disappointment that comes at middle age —

*10,000 oxen might turn their heads inquiringly
at such a load.*

Prospects? First financial humiliation,
then ruin,

in a world composed of once-familiar objects
left to gather strangeness in the rain.

Easy to forget all thought is detail,
fashioned out of wood and iron,

when those who imagine
they drag civilization forward,

living in a self-imposed obscurity,
erect implausible schemata and,

beneath their shadows,
endlessly complain about their heavy loads.

Still, I want to know what's going to happen
outside these walls after I've gone.

Lay me out under one of those blue July skies
that make me think of being newly born.

Tell them it's because I devoted my life to leisure and study,
because I'd want to see, for one last time, the great rooves of the
         Forbidden City.

Then stand me in an official's hat under the six-fingered maple
and, so the ink dries quickly, write my name in water on stone.

Notes to the Poems (From the Late Tang)

Drifting dust on all sides.
Drifting, lost on all sides.

First a famous emperor's calligraphy, and then a poet's,
written from the farthest reaches of the empire, out of exile.

The character for heart:
a one-inch square where ancient days have vanished into the world.

This past is another's future, this future another's past:
either can be split along the grain for firewood.

I see them gathered on the old silk scrolls,
poring over yet more ancient histories.

All that was once so mighty, seemingly invincible.
Vast monuments to public greatness that flowered once, littering the cities.

Now, like aging exiles, no more than the remnants of an age that clamors
impotently from offshore, vowing always to return home.

Out of the mountains then, mountains. Out of the fire, fire.
Out of the mind, snow.

These are the blurred, virtually anonymous forms
that people the landscape.

They rise and fall,
like columns of troops, or columns of smoke.

The fisherman, as always, is hidden from the fish.
The rider from the mournful hooves of the horse, and its willful rambling.

The unnaturalness of the frontier wind
that stirs these nomad instruments

is always in my ears. I see it already
entering the garden,

beheading the roses,
while I climb the steps to the music of small birds.

Small Wild Goose Pavilion (An Introduction to Wang Wei)

If one particle of dust is raised, the state comes into being.
If one particle of dust is spared, the state must die.

But mountains and rivers survive.
I see the road, the piles of dusty pomegranates —
and the hands of peasants bleeding
where the sutras say to look for them to bleed.

The Wall is to the north, and fallen into disrepair,
and all the bones of those who built it
swim up lazily toward the surface of that stream
at dusk, as if to feed.

A wooden comb, the miniature funeral cortege,
immortalize some unknown functionary.
The sprawl of factories as night descends and
all the city's lights wink on across the plain.

Across the sea of heaven,
boats set sail;
daybreak sees the characters returning to their stele
in the cool snail-shade.

Above the streets, the towers built to house the sutras,
translated and brought back from India, still rise,
the cool courtyards rustling with the shade of scholar trees
so old Wang Wei once strolled beneath their leaves.

I sit beneath them and the book falls open in my lap:
An ancient tree once grew in the precincts of my hand,
it reads, *too big for little men,*
but now the heart is riddled with ants.

In the Forbidden City, I Went to See the Marble Staircase That Reputedly Leads to Heaven and Was for the Emperor's Use Alone. Having Finally Found It, With Its Coiling Dragons, Clouds and Mountains, I Walked Over to One of the Green Areas of the Great Palace Compound and, Looking Down Onto the Blue Rooves, Remembering the Three Gorges, Wrote This Poem (An Introduction to Du Fu)

Morning is the first of the three awesome gorges
that begin at Guizhou.
The sounds of fishermen at work, at noon, along the riverbanks.
The spirit of a wronged ghost rising like a stormcloud
from the shattered legbone of a long-dead laborer
that juts up from the ruins of the Great Wall
far away, and to the north of here.

The Wall extends, as one can see
only from space, ten thousand *li*.
Impossible to comprehend in scale —
of the total population, one in five
actually engaged in its construction.
From the villages, and young men mostly, at the pleasure
of an emperor's decree.

Now I have left, I see again
the red and bronze gates of the fabled city.
Great stone cisterns coiled about with dragons,
and the dogs of heaven in a circle round the emperor's knee.
The splendors of the capital. But now,
as if still looking, at the same time,
from Guizhou,

a cool breeze blowing on the river and,
along the shore, the chugging of our engine fades,
the in-vain-colored oriole casts its lovely sounds
into reflections gathered up like bolts of silk

before the worn prows of the fishing boats
that ply their trade along the river and return,
as night falls, to the villages, and home.

I want to say the time for awe is past,
the veneration of a way of being
held up like a mirror in a kind of hopeful vanity
towards a time that never was
— rain on the leaves of the plantain,
white ghost lilies that the moon has opened at the trellis,
and the sounds of autumn, faintly incandescent.
But the road runs north from here, toward the frontier,

as it always has — once clogged with carts and peasants
while the wealthy practiced their refinements.
Now, among the flowering pavilions,
bronze stars rise at dusk,
the shadows of the temples, old before their time,
reach halfway to the cypresses, whose boughs are bent
beneath their rooves as if in imitation.

In the chronicles it states one hundred thousand men or more
were buried in the Wall, while countless others had to labor on,
unable to return home to their villages for decades,
arriving finally to find their wives and children old.
I have seen the fruits of all that labor crumbled into disrepair.
Also the satin chair to which an emperor retired, composing there
a famous set of verses to be dropped into the river as an offering.

Excuse these struggles. No means having come into existence
to resist the passage of imperial decrees.
It is said that one dynasty was destroyed by conversation
and another by convention,
and it may be so,
but in the old city now, night has fallen,
soon the gorges will be flooded,

and no image resembles sound,
no sound amazes the eye.

The Lotus (An Introduction to Wang Wei)

Even the lotus is a kind of bait:
the waxen flowers that float, unchanging,
on a mirrored, stationary world.

But all things lie,
the scholars poled across in barges
disturb the placid imagery.

Seen from a distance,
each year is a small cottage
from which we set out

in a universe where rain, mountains and cloud
eliminate salvation.
The body, the senses,

are leaves of the self.
That when the wind blows, shiver,
when the deluge passes, are wet with rain.

Late Summer (From the Late Tang)

"Reprieved by laziness", I think, "the garden of the afternoon
lies open." Beneath the pines
the sky revolving hangs as if suspended in the breeze of thirteen
                centuries.
A blue so bright that
small transparent creatures passing through it
flash into existence, and then out again.
Their dreams, too, are not tranquil.
I see them, like the past, divided endlessly —
against the sky above Chang'an.
The murmur of the pines.
Wang Wei, Du Fu, Meng Jiao.
Li Bai, Du Mu, Li He.

惡詩皆得官

好詩空抱山

Long Ago (An Introduction to Du Fu)

No market for awe.
No moon in a river of mud.

The moon in a river of mud —
ignorant, ashamed, on foot.

Once poetry was a form of government.
Now drifting, memorized by rain.

Now drifting, now adrift.

Rain (From the Late Tang)

Personal names, place names, brief, desirous —

like rain in a purely honorary time.

The cat calls: someone looking endlessly
among the fallen worlds.

In this world too beautiful to be true,
and too beautiful not to be true.

As if the faint aroma of a logic floated —
or some argument were being made.

What if these words became the rain,
and then the rain ended.

As though I were thinking them (of course),
but they all seemed equally beautiful,

equally distant,
as though they weren't mine at all —

Title and Subject (An Introduction to Du Fu)

I have written this book out of a sense of order:
people either know all or know only a little.
I have taken the poems and pounded them,
or hoarded them, like corn, in cribs.
Their form is neither beautiful nor pleasing,
but patient enough —
like the end of the will, which is the gateway
through which generations pass.

Now the pleasures are over.
The centuries become schoolbooks.
I make no apology. Here as elsewhere,
I do not propose to undertake the impossible task
of trying to explain in language
the meanings I have made.

Standing Straight (From the Late Tang)

This world is too beautiful to be true,
and too beautiful not to be true —
but life does not depend on truth.

Too beautiful to be true,
and too beautiful not to be true —
so that the world still marvels
at so many with so many designs on it,
so many plans to embellish it against its will.

This is the cypress that was old before Kunming temple was built.
Its roots are like cast bronze footings.
All the ministers who sat in its shade
have had their own appointments and are gone,
but the tree is still cherished.
The moon emerges from its branches,
eager to communicate, white as mountains.

White Peony (From the Late Tang)

Betrayed by hallucinatory love,
she clothes herself in a life of pure sensation.
White silk. The vague and fitful heart.

Is it the flowers or remorse then?
Is the day past or future?

Like the moon she waits for fifteen hundred years,
like water where the rain dwells. She lies down.
Rhyme and iambics are brought to their knees.

Kind language, meaning all that it can mean.

Hard Years (An Introduction to Wang Wei)

I have a cottage at Year's End:
a bridge there links the empty forest with white clouds.

Another one runs to the peopled world.
It's my path to the purging and meddling.

Take either one, but don't look down:
the water of those years drowned so many.

Sometimes I think to leave this world —
but I don't know which bridge might lead to you,

and you and I,
we are the only ones left alive.

Mountain Range (An Introduction to Wang Wei)

In its range and beauty, and from a distance,
the desire to be without desire looks like a mountain range.

A blue haze, almost smoky, wraps the things of this world.
The body, the senses:

nothing you'll ever read could move you from this world.
Sometimes I'm tempted to fill it with emotion,

the way as a bureaucrat I filled each day with self-importance.
I suppose salvation is always to be found elsewhere,

only there's no human voice now,
and the empty forest isn't empty, it's full of crickets.

Preparing to Leave Guizhou (An Introduction to Du Fu)

The voices come from all directions now.
What's wrong? They're too quiet,
they know what it is they have to say.
Had I passed the imperial exams, would things have been different?
Would my wife have had more to eat?
Would my son have survived?
Would I have been satisfied with that kind of plenty,
and in the end settled for less, not even knowing,
but with less pain to others?
What do I long for now
besides horses, eras, and countries —
long banquet tables groaning with plates of
snake and hummingbird tongue,
all gorged on by the powerful.
Once I had a teacher; now everyone is dead.
The wind dies too, though there's no one left
who would say it lives.
If you want to visit this village,
you'll have to ask the nuns at the base of the hill.
They're canny: they'll give wrong directions,
from which you'll have to decipher
the true ones. When you get here,
we can sit together on my little mat.
We'll invite the neighbor over, and make him
drink my cheap wine. But don't bring
"it" with you, the world, when you come.

Sun in the Eye (An Introduction to Wang Wei)

Seeing the pines by the trail bleed imperial yellow,
like rain in a purely honorary time, I thought:
so, now I can devote myself to pleasure, and an end I cannot see.

From here it seemed
the future lay open, if only momentarily.

But there were horses stilled in the high passes.
We passed them casually enough, each to the other completely
                    inconsequential,
like clouds passing overhead as one is drifting off at night.

If there is any particular meaning to this
it is perhaps that what there is escapes me,
or that there is no true meaning,

only the great blue wall of the sky,
against which fidelity to the image is impossible.

Thinking of Suzhou (An Introduction to Du Fu)

The centuries are
set in stone, or lost in gardens, to elude us —
so why not take to the road again,
like those before us,
stumbling and forgetting, as friendship allows?

The road is paved with broken teapots and ricebowls
from here to the capital. A stop to rest means
rain on the shoes, and contemplation.
Each grassblade is the grave of a vanished immortal,
sipped at by beetles.

Thinking of Suzhou,
the rain that blew once in shimmering fans
from the drip plates.
The roof tiles chipped now, and the rain
wild again, staining the mansion walls.

Fireflies (An Introduction to Wang Wei)

The creeping shadows move across the paving stones,
and once more I have taken flight from difficulty.
First the honking of the cranes, and then my mother's weeping,
though I know she is dead, and there is
nothing to it, only the sound of last night's rain.
Too lazy for old age, I've drifted again.
I mistook this existence for poetry.
And now I find myself empty-handed,
with only a name, and a few dubious imitations.

Leaving Chang'an (From the Late Tang)

This is the sound of paint on silk, that reaches to the world's end,
where the rain-soaked autumn makes its uncompleted journey into
            exile:
the camel trains set off again along the road for distant Samarkand,
still neither gone nor not gone,
so the memory of them wavers just a little in the diction of their time.
I hear the steady drumbeat of a thousand minor histories,
an emperor's disdain, a merchant's greed —
and here, too, everything remains as usual:
unhappy women leading happy dogs
and, in their wake, tall men with short cigars,
a table in a small café
where reason lays out its items and pieces,
old bits of gem and amber, silks for foreign markets,
stopping finally for the night.
Literature hates destiny,
and art hates life!
I long for that place — at the world's end, let's say,
beyond the dark green door —
where the emperor, in vain, commands the rain-soaked autumn
to begin its journey. And seeing this —
the rains beyond the pass, that is —
it seems it might at last be time
for me to take my silks and set out for the lights of distant Samarkand.

Frost (An Introduction to Du Fu)

Breath is a protest against winter —
continued over the years by way of
frost and an abiding peevishness.
The frost that forms on minds and centuries
while everything grows meekly old.

We owe our existence, as Du Fu has said,
to love and anguish.
Hands that reach out of the past
to touch what made it possible,
and draw back from the cold.

But I was determined not to take flight from that language,
a language of destruction that across a thousand years
was still shaping itself into the frost of written form —
a daughter's hunger waking in the morning to
rebellion and another day of chaos on the road.

This is to say that meaning surrounds everything.
I struggled with notes and a dictionary,
just to say that poetry need not be lost.
Words fell; one caught me by the sleeve.
It was a dead spirit, resembling the friend
whose breath gave rise to it,

but I am grateful for its touch.

Sea and Sky (An Introduction to Du Fu)

Lie down before clouds:
could be anywhere, not made by anybody's going.

Bow down among birds
pecking at coconuts, be famous first among mynahs or crows.

Then you won't need fame — or history —
the most prized possessions, as always,

being those least in need of future generations
to hand them on to.

Far below, a small storm is drenching the Pacific:
the chains of sandy blue-green atolls pass,

I drink my tea,
and bare transparent creatures,

headless,
live out their lives between two grains of sand.

Strange River (From the Late T'ang)

Gazing down into a language and literature not our own,
the dangers lie on every side, known and unknown,
with few exceptions to the rule. Neither love nor information
will bring us any nearer, and doubt makes reasonable claims.
Yet only here may we drink the water of mysterious origin
so far from the mainstream the whole looks uniform and still.
Strange river, full of images, dead women, sunken leaves,
that waver underwater, buried, where ambition lies.

Don't Wake Me Anymore (Thinking of Certain Inscriptions From the Late Tang)

Even if Chen Yuan, aroused by clear music, were to be dragged back
from death with his hair still uncombed; though Guan Yu
were to mourn again with the hard serenity of the moon —
don't wake me anymore. Sour plums for the tongue,
pine for the pine wind, bamboo for the old master.
Old-Servant-Heart, Whole-World-Plan, empty curtains
where the long winds are beginning to blow. Don't wake me again,
Chen Yuan, no more inscriptions. No paintings, Guan Yu. Instead,
may the dead mirror the living, the living mirror the dead,
let the road mirror the river, the river run like iron again.

Moon-Viewing From the Late Tang

A poem is either a poem of sorts,
or nothing, a mistake from first to last,

though existence, on occasion, speaks its feelings:
ugliness brightening the rooves of the pleasure quarter

shot through with ecstasy and
fresh, youthful hair. *Want to. Dare not.*

Wish to. Cannot. The voices are drunk
on the wedding night.

Sight, smell, flesh, tears — a thousand years
after meaning has been lost,

yet who bothers to look up?
The youthful ghosts still leaned against the

painted rail. Pleasure's
intense, invulnerable life.

A desolate world, lost in detail,
where the bronze pans set out by an emperor

to catch the dew, and immortality,
survive — and by the eastern gate,

where once again the moon has risen on Chang'an,
the bronze immortals weep, because their lords are gone.

Variation on a Few Lines by Meng Jiao (From the Late Tang)

Above the gorges, one thread of sky,
a place that the flying birds do not reach.

The color of night is rising on the road,
and still I've found no good way to live.

Strange notion, racing off
after the scent of immortality.

A human figure, moving there,
is like a tree, virtually invisible, much too human.

These are the standard views then:
a place that the flying birds do not reach,

a human figure, moving,
like a tree, the pine wind

blowing gently at each turning of the road,
morning after morning, to be close to floating fame!

Literary Criticism (An Introduction to Wang Wei)

For ten years, while the narrator lay in bed,
a plague of scholars swarmed up from the 19th Century
and out across the 20th, emerging finally into the light and tenure,
blinking their eyes and calling down
scorn upon the near and newly dead.

A sense of purposelessness filtered over the city,
"Time passing in the city is negatively framed", it said,
but this freedom was itself purposeless,
and altered that life.

It was a time of ephemera.
Flags flew at half-mast for a
disgraced president, and
quick enthusiasms were everywhere,

from the seekers after non-being and illumination,
trudging across the 19th Century
as across the vast Gobi desert,
so vast the crossing blots out even time,

to the radical pretensions of the
intellect-eoisie,
storming the barricades of the academy
with extra parentheses for the revolutionary dead.

In every decline are violent upheavals,
people like frozen meat littering the road.
The road runs from poverty to anguish, anguish to poverty,
and back again. Freedom itself is purposeless,
yellow roots and violet wind.

Those who exist in this network of allusions
live out a strange life of *sophistication* —
the "death of the author", issues of "the text" —

the glamor of a naive image whose apotheosis
is the life of revolutionary intellection —
But whatever else may form the makings of the revolution,
the chitterings and self-aggrandizements of the privileged classes
aren't a part of it.

And what if the author of the text is dead?
If the real ruler *is* the audience?
At dusk Wang Wei sets out again to walk beside the Wang River.
The shrill sound of critics rises from the hedges,
but after awhile fades into the background and is heard no more.
I am here to announce the death of the critic,
the resurrection of the book Wang Wei.
Slowly at first, I turn the pages.
I lie on a warm rock in the sun all day.
I stop at the thorn gate seized by grief.
I ask for his wooden door to be green wood again.

The Prince (An Introduction to Wang Wei)

To dream is to express everything,
the original Chinese concealed in the bark of the Buddha tree,
the weight of duty and mountains,

or the human-figured pine wind, where the rain is
laughter, or the rain, perhaps,
is rain.

Above the hills the light of evening is framed with cloud,
unchanged or changeable.
Such rare extremes —

and yet that bright star, hung aloft,
may long ago have ceased to be.
That kind of certainty is no more meaningful,

though everything may be expressed by dreaming.
The hills like darkest ink.
The text seen only by the evening.

The prince, who once was happy in these hills, can stay.

Scraps of Paper (From the Late Tang)

Avert the eyes, even a little:
and salvation's off, long gone, it's out of here:
but then, where it's said to be is always elsewhere.
So what if the gods of these poems no longer come to visit me?
This book is where they make their home,
flying to and fro in its pages
depending on whose eyes are near.
The poems themselves form the decorated border
of a country so vast even the local god
winces as he lifts his head to sip tea, like a man with a headache,
resting his eyes back on little silk pillows. After all,
on such a windy day the wind is everywhere,
and will listen to anything.
It scatters the rain, "ferries the clouds", and keeps salvation,
like an old sheet of paper, caught up in its gusts,
just out of reach.

Rereading Li Bai (From the Late Tang)

And so, at the end of discourse, I shut my gate,
and see the road run north from here.

Not the road to Shu, which is hard,
harder than climbing the blue sky —

but leading elsewhere.
Like those certain flowers that bloom at dusk,

those wild birds that forget,
at last, to go home.

Xi'an (From the Late Tang)

As a bronze bell is inscribed with
instructions for its use (and in addition, of course,
a few words of praise for the bell);

as a fragment of text, a pact entered into
by the state of Jin, lies in state now, under glass,
a small black mouth;

as ancient pictographs inscribed on oracle bones
are boiled for medicine, while words spoken only
moments ago are

bound as books, and in the old Tang capital,
stone classics, long ago erected,
serve up knowledge to the whirlwind —

these are only brief messages, intended for divination,
secrets made of wood and iron,
hardly legible.

They are not to be studied, or copied.

The Gates of Chu

When stones opposite the openings of side-streets
scare away demons, what would an actual god be like?
Not the ascent of a mountain, seen or not seen,
not elaborate rules arrayed around us like the
distant, fixed stars in a cosmos
wheeling overhead each night.
Beauty is concentrated by order and wildness.
The moon climbing into the arms of her daughter.
Houses and roads that pass in and out of existence
not knowing we have already gone because it is late April
and the year at last is beautiful again.
Now I have come to the gates of Chu,
the village where likeness was born.
I imagine the crimson terraces,
the northern deserts stretched as though before her eyes,
but only the Green Tomb is left,
as solitary as before dusk,
the houses of the great families finally emptied.
Everything is ultimately indescribable.
Only the roar of existence,
like a dish of dark red agate
out of which a flame,
continuously fed by strips of satin,
blazes with a god-like mettlesomeness,
a kingfisher brushing the sky,
a paradox the centuries will multiply steadily.
And yet to look at anything (as a god might)
when there's so much to forget.
I look at my hand, and it's the end of the world.

Afterword

The first collection of Tang Dynasty poetry I came across was called *The Jade Mountain*, assembled and translated by Witter Bynner and Kiang Kang-hu, first published in 1929, and then again, in somewhat cheaper (and hence more accessible) form, in paperback, in 1964. This was in my local library, where books of poetry were rare, and my interest in them not high, since they ran mostly to "well-loved" anthologies, amidst which were scattered, in an act (presumably) either of public-spiritedness or charity, various bits of local arcana. To find a book of poetry, then, that was neither mimeographed, nor a great unwieldy leather tome — a book consisting entirely of poems translated from a foreign language, the originals of which had been written (not to mention annotated, reproduced, and argued over) centuries before my own language was even born, by writers whose names I was at sea pronouncing and had certainly never heard of; whose cover, moreover, was already curled a bit and felted at the upper corner and, though of recent vintage, had not one, but three, small pages glued into its backing, the third already half-full of recent due-date stamps, sometimes in red, sometimes in pale blue — was a great novelty. I was living, at the time, in a house in which there were bookshelves and books in every room except the bathrooms, the sort of house where books might be picked up briefly and wandered with, and so end up migrating anywhere. Coming home from the library, taking the books I'd brought back with me up to my room, I realized suddenly the book whose turquoise spine had stood among the other duller and more book-ish colors, for a year or more now, on the small shelf set into the shallow alcove, into which the headboard of my bed was also set, was none other than *The Jade Mountain*, the book I'd "discovered" so excitedly that afternoon. How it had got there, or even when, I don't know, though I do remember getting ready for sleep and gazing at its turquoiseness each night, long before that afternoon.

In what in English we still call Mandarin, but which since 1949, in China, has been called "putonghua" ("the common language", though in fact it is a dialect of the north), the color turquoise is known as qing lü, or "natural-color green", qing meaning "natural (color)"; lü, green. Qing hai: the blue sea; qing shan: the green mountains; qing ye: the black night. It is as if all things have their own "natural" color: the green of the mountains (that might, to us, be grey, or blue), the blue of the sea (that might, also, be green), the gloom of a car accident that is black (but might instead be that deep almost sweet blue of certain paintings) when one is lying in the hospital, having just come close to death. So natural green would be as good a color as any to describe those poems, most of them now more than 1200 years old, but still strangely fresh, as if waiting for us to come upon them again.

This note to the reader begins with a vignette which is, in fact, not one memory, but a composite of three — and this, as well, is how the poems in this volume came to be composed. All the poems collected here were written collaboratively, and are derived (for the most part), in varying degrees, from other texts. If *The Jade Mountain* was an early talisman, the writings whose presences can be discerned here were less talismans than alternate topographies, places where we might wander a little — exploring, daydreaming, playing, resting now and then by a stream, or under a tree, becoming lost — until we knew them as (though starting with a map) one comes to know a piece of land: individually (and hence idiosyncratically), locally, with (now and then) a love of small backwaters others might disdain; above all, with a magpie's delight in what is bright and lovely. Our sources, or sounding boards, our landscapes, in the end, were many and varied. Critical introductions to translations of the original Chinese; the varying translations and prose glosses themselves; some of the poems in the original classical Chinese (or as close to the originals as current scholarship is able to agree on); in one case, the writings of someone unconnected with any of this (Jean Baudrillard); and finally, the felt but insubstantiable influences (Montale is one, Ovid another, Mathew Arnold a third) whose diction or imagery seemed to hover near certain of the texts as we composed them. All of these were present; all had their influences.

In some cases we might see, before our very eyes as it were, a word or phrase take up the brief flash of another, paragraphs or pages separate, as if a spark had jumped suddenly across the intervening spaces. In others, a paragraph or passage, sometimes as little as a single syllable (a phenomenon well-known to writers of renga) might serve as a kind of slow tinder, igniting finally something very different from the original.

These poems, then, *grow out of* our reading of the Tang Dynasty poets
(Wang Wei, Du Fu, Li Bai, Li He, Meng Jiao ...). They may be thought
of, in some sense, as free variations — sometimes on the original poems
and translations, sometimes on elements of the critical commentaries of
the translators, sometimes on a combination of sources — the result
being, we hope, some analogue, appropriate to our time and culture, of
the high degree of allusiveness of classical Chinese poetry, especially that
of the High Tang. Certain poems (such as "The Constellations", which
can be read as a rather loose variation on Du Fu's "Zeng Wei Ba Chu
Shi", translated by David Hawkes as "To the Recluse Wei Pa") can indeed
be thought of as free variations in a more traditional sense — in the
spirit, perhaps, of Lowell's "variations" on Montale. Often, however, the
poems are sparked off by what might, from the viewpoint, say, of a
reader skimming the original for content rather than texture, best be
called a random selection of words and phrases, i.e., a set of elements
scattered throughout the original with no apparent connection, in the
sense of the logic and needs of the original piece. These poems, then, are
not "variations" (in the usual sense) of anything — they do not seek to
follow, however loosely, the emotional, rhetorical, or logical framework
of any particular poem, translation, or introduction. They are instead
(for the most part) like "ordinary" poems, that is, constructed out of our
individual/collective impulses and experiences, only, through our
interests, inclinations, and the process of composition, colored faintly
throughout by our immersion in that literature, its tradition, and, of
course, the work of those translators — much as the work of poets like
Wang Wei and Du Fu, though in no sense an imitation or recapitulation
of what went before them, nonetheless bears the imprint, both explicit
(i.e., deliberate) and implicit, of the long tradition, stretching back to
The Book of Songs, in which they were immersed and came into
existence as poets.

This, then, in the end, is neither a work of scholarship, nor (with one
exception) of translation, but a book of poems. The poems here, in some
important sense, have only a tangential relationship to those other texts.
And yet, reading the Tang Dynasty poets, as well as the works of
translation and commentary, has fed into the process of writing here in a
larger way than is usual — reading being a part of experience but, in
this case, a larger-than-usual component of the experience that went

into the writing of these poems. Harry Mathews, talking of his work with the Oulipo, has said that the point of writing with constraints is not so much in the fact of the constraints themselves as in, having done so, finding oneself suddenly again on "home ground". A home ground whose existence might have otherwise remained unknown. "Here the eye ultimately composes itself", writes Thomas Jefferson, in his early jottings, collected as *Notes on the State of Virginia*, "and that way too the road happens actually to lead."

In writing this book, our aim has not been to re-present as poetry the views and works of other authors, and the various authors we have read and re-read shouldn't be blamed for the meaning or quality of anything that appears here — though the translators and commentators among them should be recognized and thanked for the work they have done in bringing into the English language a sense of the greatness of the Tang Dynasty poetry. In some sense the poems of this book are no different from any others: they are *sparked off* by something. In another, however, they are different because, at least in some cases, more evidently than is the case for most poetry, they are alloys — that is, they contain certain metals which are clearly not of our own invention. One might say that they are "intended" to have a secondariness about them: to succeed as original inventions of our own and yet still have about them the perfume of some "elsewhere" from which they might be said to come. If (as one of the poems says) for the poets of the Tang Dynasty, "the use and reuse of traditional Chinese poetry" represented a way of allying themselves with the long tradition of that poetry, and, at the same time, "honoring the masters", one could equally well see, in that combination of fondness and hubris, an admission that it is impossible to fully enter a text (even one's own), no matter the language or century. As the subtitles to the poems (perhaps repetitively) insist, it is nonetheless possible, through reading and re-reading, to find a place for oneself, to stand, as it were, as if perpetually stuck, in some doorway which opens out onto those great works.

In an afterword — that is, in retrospect — it's hard to emphasize with sufficient clarity the indeliberateness of what went before; and yet the indeliberateness here is the same as that which attends the writing of all true poetry. If we have wandered a little, then that, in our opinion, is as it should be. We would like to end as we began, with Wang Wei, poet and bureaucrat, first in his own words, and then in a translation of our own making:

此　名　偶　不　前　宿　惟　老
心　字　被　能　身　世　有　來
還　本　世　舍　應　謬　老　懶
不　皆　人　餘　畫　詞　相　賦
知　是　知　習　師　客　隨　詩

From **Six Casually Written Poems** (No. 6)

Old age comes, and I've grown lazy about writing poems.
Only old age now, so we follow each other around.
In this long life, mistakenly a poet —
in a past life, it would seem, a painter also.
Unable to give up these remaining habits,
I happen to be known to the world.
There are those who know my name,
but not this heart.

Notes on the Text

A Note on Orthography and Pronunciation

No reader of a book of poetry in English can be expected to digest the names of Chinese people and places in their original written form. In order to name such people and places we have, therefore, had to decide on a convention for transliteration. Partly because it is the system with which we are most familiar, and hence most comfortable, partly because it is the one in use throughout mainland China, and partly because it is visually more compact than common, older alternatives, we have opted for the pinyin system of romanization, for simplicity printed here without tone marks. In most cases the pronunciations suggested to a native English speaker by this truncated form of pinyin are a good approximation to those of modern Mandarin (though shorn of its tones). A few elements of the system, however, are likely to cause some confusion to the uninitiated. Since this confusion could, on occasion, create sonic effects we neither intended nor would be happy with, we provide the reader with a short guide to the less obvious aspects of pinyin pronunciation. In doing so we hope, at least, that the names of some of our favorite poets may survive the perils of the passage from Chinese to English relatively intact, and perhaps arouse in the ear of the reader some of the same fondness we ourselves feel in hearing them. The 'x' is a soft 's' sound, made with the tongue pressed against the back of the bottom teeth, hence slightly toward 'sh' (more strongly so in southern dialects). The 'j' sound is similarly softened, in contrast to 'zh', which is a somewhat harder version, akin to the first syllable of 'jury', made with the tongue curled toward the back of the mouth. A similar distinction exists between the soft 'ch' sound, represented by 'q', and the hard version, 'ch', made with tongue curled back and pronounced something like 'churn' with most of the 'r' and all of the 'n' removed. The 'c' is pronounced like the 'ts' of 'its'. The vowel sounds all have natural analogues in English: 'a' is pronounced like the 'a' in 'awe', the 'o' of 'dong' like the 'oo' in 'loon', 'ai' like 'eye', 'i' like the 'i' of 'machine', 'ou' like the 'o' of 'yo', 'ei' like the 'ay' of 'say', 'ui' like 'way', and the 'e' (as in Li He and Meng Jiao) like the 'e' in 'inert'. The reader should bear in mind that modern Mandarin and Tang Dynasty Chinese pronunciations differ by more than a thousand years of usage and evolution. Much of the old system of pronunciation has, in fact, been lost, and what *is* known about it has been reconstructed by scholars, often via studies of the rhyme patterns of poems of that era. The Mandarin pronunciation underlying pinyin may recast some of the poets into forms less familiar to the reader; for those readers, Li Bai is Li Po; Du Fu, Tu Fu; Meng Jiao, Meng Chiao; Du Mu, Tu Mu; and Li He, Li Ho. For ourselves, we hear throughout the Mandarin pronunciation, and the music of the poems is constructed with these pronunciations in mind.

A Note on Some Relevant Historical Facts

While we would hope that all the poems could be read and appreciated without recourse to supplementary historical information, a few facts may prove of some extracurricular interest to the reader. Chang'an was the main capital of the Tang Dynasty (618-906 AD), Luoyang the eastern capital. A good portion of Chang'an survives in the center of modern Xi'an. Guizhou is on the middle Yangtze, at the entrance to the Three Gorges. Du Fu spent two years in Guizhou shortly before his death and wrote many of his most famous poems there. The Three Gorges are currently in the process of being flooded by a massive hydro-electric project. Wang Wei (699-761 or 701-759), Du Fu (712-770) and Li Bai (701-762) all lived through the catastrophic rebellion led by the mercenary general An Lushan, which lasted from 755-763, and devastated most of the country. All three suffered severe hardship during this period. In Tang Dynasty China, the government was run by scholar bureaucrats, and the ability to write various forms of poetry was considered an important skill, one tested as part of the *jinshi* (presented scholar) examinations which determined whether or not one would be allowed to enter the bureaucracy and, if so, how high the position in the bureaucracy might be. Despite this, only Wang Wei managed to achieve high office. The other poets who make appearances in this book (Meng Jiao (751-814), Li He (791-817) and Du Mu (803-852)) all lived in the aftermath of the An Lushan rebellion, in an era that felt its own golden age had passed.

A Note on Sources

The lines beginning the four sections of the book are by Meng Haoran, Du Fu, Li He and Meng Jiao, in that order. The poem "The Clouds" is a loose variation on "Li Ren Xing" ("The Ballad of the Lovely Women") by Du Fu, in the David Hawkes translation; "The Constellations" on "Zeng Wei Ba Chu Shi" ("To the Recluse Wei Pa"), also by Du Fu, and also in the David Hawkes translation. "Storm Lanterns" is a variation, in some sense, on both Du Fu's work and life, as a whole; it consists of thirty-some first lines (or portions thereof), sometimes with minor modifications, as contained in the David Hinton translation. "Variation on a Few Lines by Meng Jiao" is a variation on first lines by Meng Jiao, in the A.C. Graham translation. Similarly, "Another Universe" works with material from the essay "On Seduction" by Jean Baudrillard; "Introduction to Du Fu" with material from David Hinton's introduction to *The Selected Poems of Tu Fu*; and "Convicted of Greatness Twelve Centuries After His Death, Wang Wei is Imprisoned in a Cage of Jargon", with material from the introduction to *Laughing Lost in the Mountains — Selected Poems of Wang Wei*, by Tony Barnstone, Willis Barnstone and Xu Haixin (which, our title aside, provides an elegant and illuminating discussion of Wang Wei's work in relation to that of poets from the European tradition). The translation of the sixth of the "Six Casually Written Poems" contained in the Afterword is by Pain Not Bread and based on the version contained in *Wang Wei Shi Xuan*. For other translations of this poem see *The Poetry of Wang Wei: New Translations and Commentary* by Pauline Yu, and *Wang Wei* by Marsha L. Wagner.

A Further Note on Sources

Two groups of books were critical to the writing of this one. The first consists of those works which, as already noted, became our alternate topographies. Various elements of these books resonate throughout and/or are echoed in our own. The second group consists of those which, while not "primary sources", nonetheless lent some crucial nuance, understanding, or fragrance to the composition of the poems. We wish to thank all of the authors for providing us with an opportunity to drink with them, however briefly, from those various streams.

The first group:

Barnstone, Tony; Willis Barnstone, and Xu Haixin. *Laughing Lost in the Mountains — Selected Poems of Wang Wei*. Beijing: Panda Books, 1989.

Beaudrillard, Jean. "On Seduction", in *Jean Beaudrillard: Selected Writings*. Edited and introduced by Mark Poster. Stanford: Stanford University Press, 1988.

Geddes, Gary; and George Liang. *I Didn't Notice the Mountain Growing Dark: Poems of Li Pai and Tu Fu*. Dunvegan, ON: Cormorant Books, 1986.

Graham, A.C. *Poems of the Late Tang*. London: Penguin Books, 1977.

Hawkes, David. *A Little Primer of Tu Fu*. Hong Kong: Renditions Paperbacks, 1990.

Hinton, David. *The Selected Poems of Tu Fu*. New York: New Directions, 1989.

Wang Wei. *Wang Wei Shi Xuan*. Hong Kong: Da Guang Chu Ban She, 1973.

The second group:

Abe Masao. *A Study of Dogen: His Philosophy and Religion*. Edited by Stephen Heine. Albany: State University of New York Press, 1992.

Birch, Cyril. *Anthology of Chinese Literature: From Early Times to the Fourteenth Century*. New York: Grove Press, 1965.

Bynner, Witter; and Kiang Kang-hu. *The Jade Mountain: A Chinese Anthology*. Garden City, NY: Doubleday & Company, Inc., 1964.

Fairbank, John King. *China: A New History*. Cambridge, MA: The Belknap Press of Harvard University Press, 1992.

Graham, Dorothy. *Chinese Gardens: Gardens of the Contemporary Scene*. New York: Dodd, Mead and Co., 1938.

Ito Teijii. *Space and Illusion in the Japanese Garden*. New York: Weatherhill, 1973.

Kuck, Loraine E. *The Art of Japanese Gardens*. New York: The John Day Co., 1940.

Liu Guojun and Zheng Rusi. *The Story of Chinese Books*. Translated by Zhou Yicheng. Beijing: Foreign Languages Press, 1985.

Liu Wu-chi and Irving Lo. *Sunflower Splendor: Three Thousand Years of Chinese Poetry*. Bloomington: Indiana University Press, 1975.

Miyazaki Ichisada. *China's Examination Hell: The Civil Service Examinations of Imperial China*. Translated by Conrad Schirokauer. New Haven: Yale University Press, 1981.

Nakata Yujiro. *Chinese Calligraphy: A History of the Art of China*. Translated and adapted by Jeffrey Hunter. New York: Weatherhill, 1982.

Owen, Stephen. *The Great Age of Chinese Poetry: The High T'ang*. New Haven: Yale University Press, 1981.

Owen, Stephen. *Traditional Chinese Poetry and Poetics: Omen of the World*. Madison: University of Wisconsin Press, 1985.

Porter, Bill. *Road to Heaven: Encounters with Chinese Hermits*. San Francisco: Mercury House, 1993.

Sekida Katsuki. *Two Zen Classics: Mumonkan and Hekiganroku*. New York: Weatherhill, 1977.

Slawson, David A. *Secret Teachings in the Art of Japanese Gardens*. Tokyo & New York: Kodansha International, 1987.

Wagner, Marsha L. *Wang Wei*. Boston: Twayne Publishers, 1981.

Wu, John C.H. *The Golden Age of Zen*. New York: Doubleday, 1996.

Xue Tou. *The Blue Cliff Record*. Translated by Thomas and J.C. Cleary. Boulder: Shambhala, 1977.

Yang Xiangyi, and Gladys Yang. *Poetry and Prose of the Tang and Song*. Beijing: Chinese Literature, 1984.

Yu, Pauline. *The Poetry of Wang Wei: New Translations and Commentary*. Bloomington: Indiana University Press, 1980.

Acknowledgements

Thanks to the following journals in which versions of many of the poems first appeared: *Brick* ("A Little Primer of Du Fu", "Mountains and Rivers", "The Constellations"); *Canadian Literature* ("Continuous Elegy", "Breath"); *Capilano Review* ("Storm Lanterns", "Crows", "Standing Straight", "Forbidden City", "Still Evening", "Credo: Deep South Mountain", "The Gown of a Dead Emperor", "Strange River", "Mountain Range"); *The Fiddlehead* ("Fragmentary Impromptu", "Fireflies", "Small Wild Goose Pavillion", "Sea and Sky", "Variation on a Few Lines by Guan Yu"); *The Malahat Review* ("Introduction to the Introduction to Wang Wei", "Cooling Off", "Uneventful Life", "The Old Man in the Mountain", "A Life of Contemplation", "Convicted of Greatness Twelve Centuries After His Death, Wang Wei is Imprisoned in a Cage of Jargon", "Winter Night", "Cloud Music", "As Buddha Did", "Wang River" (published as "Politics Never Tamed the Angel"), "Introduction to Du Fu", "The Written Character", "Literary Criticism", "Sixty Days of Rain", "Peace Road Mountain", "Sky", "The Prince", "Every Shade of Friendship", "The Rise and Fall of Human Breath", "Another Universe", "Title and Subject", "Drunken Battles", "The Clouds", "Variation on a Few Lines by Meng Jiao", "Rereading Li Bai", "Notes to the Poems", "Lazy Afternoon, Thinking About Certain Famous Lines From the Late Tang", "Late Summer", "A Dream", "Friendship", "Snow-Viewing Room", "The News", "Scraps of Paper", "The Gates of Chu"); *Matrix* ("Bitter Heart", "Translation", "Frost", "Sun in the Eye", "Rain", "Water Chestnut Stems"); *Nimrod* ("White Peony", "Worldly Noise", "Old Prose", "A History of the Late Tang", "Moon-Viewing From the Late Tang", "The Transmission of Salt"); *Prism International* ("Sleep", "Good Daughter"); *The River Review* ("Long Ago", "The Shadows of Plum Trees", "Spring", "The Lotus"); *Text: zeitschrift für literaturen* ("Thinking of Suzhou", "In the Forbidden City, I Went to See the Marble Staircase That Reputedly Leads to Heaven and...").

A sequence entitled "Introduction to the Introduction to Wang Wei" was awarded *The Malahat Review* long poem prize in 1993, and work published in *Prism International* the Earle Birney Prize for 1999.

Special thanks to Tsau Shuying and Zeng Li for their generosity in allowing us to take part in their Mandarin courses, and for their unflagging energy, especially in putting up with our persistent questions on usage, the answers to which were invaluable to us in composing this book, but the posing of which often led well outside the usual course content. Thanks also to the Toronto Zen Centre; and to Manly Johnson and Fran Ringold, both for their hospitality and for access to the Manly Johnson Private Lending Library of Chinese Literature.

"I keep thinking of Antonioni: when asked why he wanted to do something — I forget what, and in what film — he said 'because it's technically sweet'. *Tecnicamente dolce*."